LOOk Closer

Sea creatures

DK

LONDON, NEW YORK, MUNICH,
MELBOURNE, and DELHI

Text by Sue Malyan
Editor Caroline Bingham
Senior art editor Janet Allis
Publishing manager Susan Leonard
Managing art editor Clare Shedden
Jacket design Simon Oon
Picture researcher Sarah Mills
Production Luca Bazzoli
DTP Designer Almudena Díaz

First American Edition, 2005

Published in the United States by
DK Publishing, Inc., 375 Hudson Street,
New York, New York 10014

05 06 07 08 09   10 9 8 7 6 5 4 3 2 1

Copyright © 2005 Dorling Kindersley Limited

A Cataloging-in-Publication record for this book
is available from the Library of Congress.

ISBN 0-7566-1431-7

Color reproduction by Colourscan, Singapore
Printed and bound in China by Hung Hing

Discover more at
www.dk.com

Contents

Look for us. We will show you the size of every animal in this book.

Mobile home

This hermit crab drags its home wherever it goes. It finds a shell to live in, then hides inside with just its head and front legs poking out.

This hermit crab's body reaches up to 4 in (10 cm) in length. As it grows, it finds larger shells to move into.

This shell once belonged to a whelk. It was just the right size, so I moved in.

I can see all around because my eyes are on stalks.

munch munch

Mmm, a dead fish—just what I wanted for breakfast.

Did you know...

... If a hermit crab is scared, it hides in its shell. It uses its biggest pincer to nip an attacker.

An inky trail

Whoosh! An octopus has been startled, so it has squirted a cloud of black ink into the water. Now it shoots off to hide in its home under a pile of rocks.

This common octopus is 3 ft (1 m) long.

swish

swoosh

I suck in water, then squirt it out of this funnel to push me along.

I use my arms to walk and to catch crabs and shellfish for my dinner.

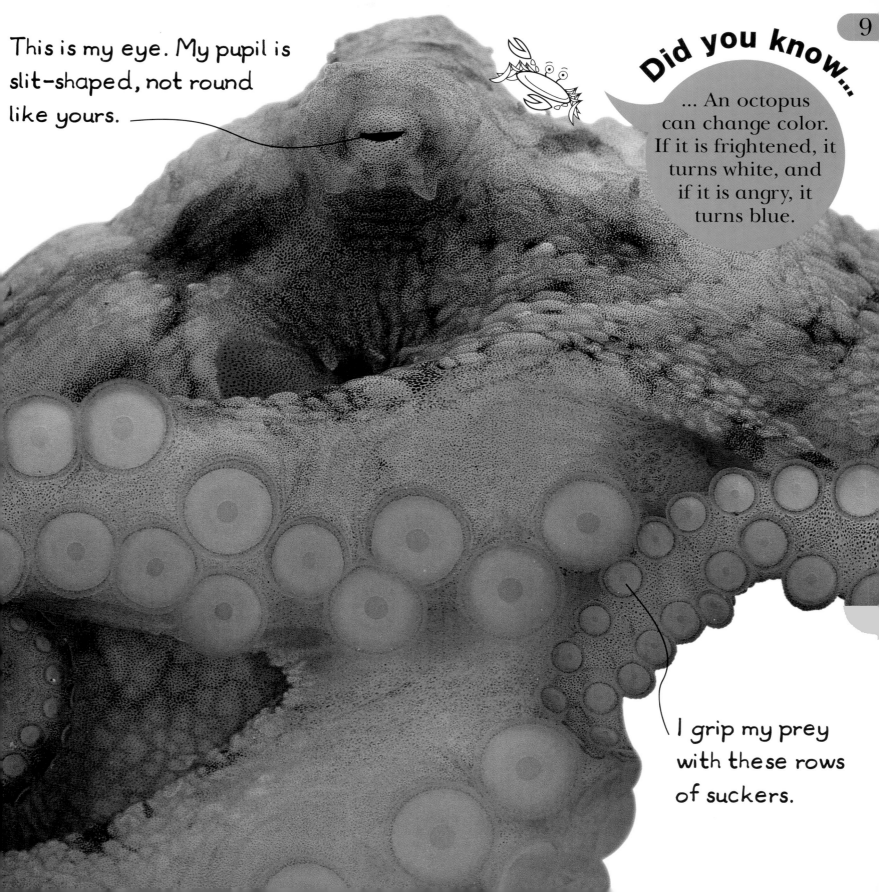

Feeling my way

This strawberry shrimp lives on a coral reef, hiding among the corals or in a burrow in the sand. Its long feelers, or antennae, help it find food.

nip nip

I use my claws for picking up food and digging in the sand. If I lose a claw, I can grow another one.

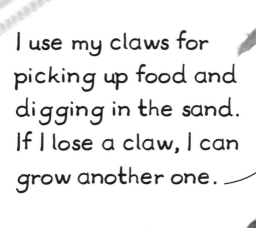

This shrimp is 2 in (5 cm) long. It is also called a blood or fire shrimp.

Crusty crab

Scuttling around a rock pool, a pie-crust crab is looking for food. It gets its name from the top part of its shell, which looks like the pastry on a pie.

An adult pie-crust crab measures about 6 in (15 cm) across its shell. That's about the size of your hand.

The colors of my shell help me hide among the pebbles.

crunch crunch crunch

I have two huge pincers for grabbing my food.

I eat shrimp and mussels.
My mouth is sharp to help me
bite through their shells.

Did you know...

... During her life, the female crab lays at least three million eggs. Only a few survive to be adults.

Look! No head!

This strange-looking animal is a sea cucumber. It has no head or eyes, just a mouth and a flexible body.

The world's largest sea cucumber is about 6 ft (2 m) long. Most are smaller. This one is about 5 in (12 cm) long.

I use the sticky tentacles around my mouth to catch my food.

My skin is tough and spiny

I feel around for tiny plants and animals.

sticky

My mouth is hidden in the middle of my tentacles.

These tiny tubes are my feet. I use them to push myself along slowly.

Did you know...

... A sea cucumber breathes through its bottom! It uses the same hole to breathe and get rid of waste.

prickly

Snappy shells

Lying on the seabed, a group of queen scallops are waiting for their next meal to float past. They trap tiny plants in the waving hairs around their shells.

I swim along by opening and shutting my shell, a bit like you clapping your hands.

snap!

Did you know...

... You can tell a scallop's age by counting the ridges on its shell. The more ridges, the older it is.

snap!

These queen scallops reach 3½ in (9 cm).

I've got rows of eyes, but I can't see well. I only sense light and things that move.

open, shut, open, shut

Look! No arms!

These seahorses live on a coral reef. They can change color to match the corals, which helps them to hide.

I hang on tight with my tail.

suck

slurp

Seahorses are small. These will grow to just 5 in (12 cm) in length.

I can suck up whole shrimp in my mouth, which is shaped like a straw.

I move around by beating the fin on my back, and I steer with two fins on my head.

I'm a grape coral. Don't touch me, or I'll sting you with my poisonous tentacles.

Did you know...

... Seahorses eat all day long. A young one can suck up as many as 3,500 shrimp in one day!

Sea stars

Did you know that if a starfish or a brittle star loses an arm, it just grows another?

This scarlet serpent brittle star's arms reach 6 in (15 cm).

I'm too spiny to eat!

wriggle wriggle wriggle

I'm called a brittle star. I move around by wriggling my arms from side to side.

I trap shrimp and other food in the spines along my arms.

Open wide!

This beautifully colored shell belongs to a giant blue clam. It can open and shut its shell, but it can't move around.

At 6 in (15 cm), this clam is quite small, but giant clams can grow to be 3 ft (1 m) across.

squirt!